D1000152

Birds

Rod Theodorou

Heinemann Library
Des Plaines, Illinois

Text designed by Celia Floyd
Illustrations by Alan Fraser
Printed in Hong Kong/China

04 03 02 01 00
10 9 8 7 6 5 4 3 2 1

The Library of Congress has cataloged the hardcover version of this book as follows:
Library of Congress Cataloging-in-Publication Data
Theodorou, Rod.
    Birds / Rod Theodorou.
        p. cm. – (Animal babies)
    Includes bibliographical references and index.
    Summary: Introduces the birth, development, care, feeding,and
characteristics of baby birds.
    ISBN 1-57572-881-8 (lib.bdg.)
    1. Birds—Infancy—Juvenile literature. 2. Parental behavior in
animals—Juvenile literature. [1. Birds. 2. Animals—Infancy.
3. Parental behavior in animals.] I. Title. II. Series: Animal
babies (Des Plaines, Ill.)
    QL676.2.T48 1999
    598.13'9—dc21   99-18053
Paperback ISBN 1-57572-541-X   CIP

Acknowledgments
The Publishers would like to thank the following for permission to reproduce photographs:
BBC/ Michael & Patricia Fogden, p. 8; Pete Oxford, p. 10; Yuri Shibnev, p. 16; Warwick Sloss, p. 23; Bruce
Coleman/John Cancalosi, p. 5; Pacific Stock, p. 6; Jen & Des Bartlett, p. 9; Kim Taylor, p. 14; George McCarthy, p.
17; NHPA/Gerald Lacz, p. 7; Pierre Petit, p. 19; E. A. Janes, p. 24; OSF/Martyn Chillmaid, p. 11; Ben Osborne, p. 15;
Ian West, p. 18; Kathie Atkinson, p. 22; Stan Osolonski, pp. 25, 27; Planet Earth/Allan Parker, p. 20; Julian
Hector, p. 26; Tony Stone/Rene Sheret, p. 12; Art Wolfe, p. 13; John Warden, p. 21.

Cover photo: Oxford Scientific Films/Robert A. Lubeck

Every effort has been made to contact copyright holders of any material reproduced in this book. Any
omissions will be rectified in subsequent printings if notice is given to the Publisher.

Some words in this book are shown in bold, **like this**. You can find out
what they mean by looking in the glossary.

Contents

Introduction 4

What Is a Bird?.....................................6

Making a Nest.....................................8

Laying Eggs 10

Hatchlings...12

Feeding the Hatchlings 14

Life in the Nest 16

Learning to Fly 18

Finding Food 20

Staying Safe......................................22

Taking Care of Baby 24

Growing Up.......................................26

Birds and Other Animals......................28

Glossary 30

More Books to Read 31

Index 32

Introduction

There are many different kinds of animals. All animals have babies. They take care of their babies in different ways.

These are the six main animal groups.

Mammal

Bird

Reptile

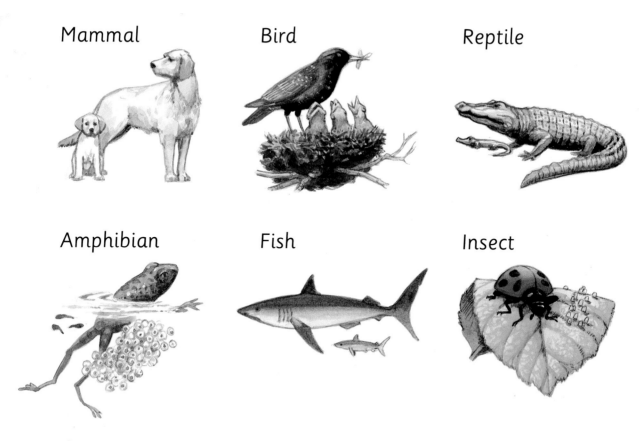

Amphibian

Fish

Insect

This book is about birds. Birds live all over the world. All female birds **lay** eggs. Baby birds **hatch** from the eggs. The babies are called chicks.

These are mute swan chicks.

What Is a Bird?

All birds:
- have two wings
- have feathers
- have a **beak**
- **hatch** from eggs

Bald eagle

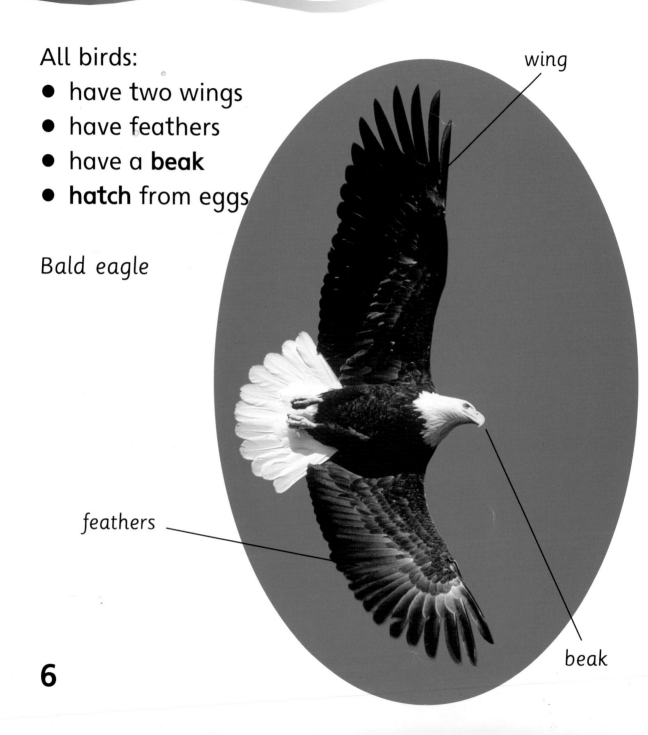

wing

feathers

beak

Most birds:

- can fly
- make a nest to **lay** their eggs in

Penguins are birds that cannot fly. They use their wings to help them swim.

Making a Nest

Most birds build nests. They build them with things they can easily find, like grass, twigs, and mud. The nest keeps the eggs warm and safe from **predators**.

This tiny hummingbird nest is made from cobwebs, leaves, and **moss**.

Some birds dig holes into the earth to make their nests. Woodpeckers peck holes in trees or **cacti** to live in. Sometimes birds move into nests that were first built by other birds.

This elf owl is nesting inside an old woodpecker hole in a cactus.

Laying Eggs

Some birds can **lay** over fifteen eggs every year. Inside some eggs are growing chicks. The egg is full of yellow **yolk** that feeds the chick.

The giant albatross lays only one egg every two years.

10

Most birds sit on their eggs to keep them warm until they **hatch**. The chick breaks open the eggshell using a sharp bump on its **beak**. This bump is called the egg tooth.

A new chick is called a **hatchling**.

Hatchlings

Some **hatchlings** are born blind and helpless.
They are small and weak and have no feathers.
Their parents have to feed them every day.

These blind sparrow hatchlings open their
beaks to be fed when they hear their parents.

12

Other kinds of chicks are born with their eyes open. They are covered with soft feathers. They can run about to find their own food.

Soon after they **hatch,** these ostrich chicks leave the nest and follow their parents.

Feeding the Hatchlings

Bird parents have to find food and bring it back to the hungry **hatchlings** all day long. Many birds **lay** eggs in the summer, because there is more food to eat.

This bird has to catch over four hundred caterpillars every day to feed its chicks.

Some **seabirds** fly out to sea to catch and eat fish. When they fly back to their nest, they bring this food back up into their **beaks** for their chicks.

This albatross chick is feeding from its parent's beak.

Life in the Nest

Sometimes the bigger chicks eat all the food. The smallest chick may die from hunger, or even be pushed out of the nest by the bigger chicks.

This golden eagle mother may bring her chick pieces of rabbits, birds, squirrels, deer, or even lambs to eat.

Some cuckoos **lay** an egg in another bird's nest. When the cuckoo chick **hatches,** it pushes the other eggs out of the nest. The mother bird thinks the cuckoo chick is her own.

This reed warbler is feeding
a huge cuckoo chick.

Learning to Fly

Soon the chicks are ready to learn to fly. They hold onto twigs and flap their wings a lot to practice and make them strong.

Pheasant chicks are ready to fly only two weeks after they **hatch.**

Some bird parents help their babies learn to fly. They fly away from the nest and call to their chicks. The chick may get food as a **reward**.

This harrier chick is learning to fly.

Finding Food

This young starling is old enough to catch its own food.

Even when they can fly, many chicks stay close to their parents. They may **beg** for food. But the parents stop feeding the chicks to make them find their own food.

Some chicks can feed themselves, but their mother shows them the best places to find food. First she calls to her chicks. They run to her and follow her.

Ducklings always follow their mother in a line.

Staying Safe

There are many animals, like foxes, that eat baby birds. Some chicks have the same color feathers as the place they live. This helps them hide away from **predators**.

These plover chicks look like pebbles.

Seabird chicks have no trees or grass to hide in. Their parents live in huge groups, called colonies, so they can help each other fight off predators.

Hundreds of gannets live in this nesting colony.

Taking Care of Baby

If a **predator** comes close to a place where birds are nesting, it may get mobbed by all the parents. This means the parents fly very close to it, even pecking at it.

These crows will mob this heron until it flies away.

Some birds **protect** their chicks by **pretending** to fly badly, as if they had a broken wing. A predator will often follow the parent, leaving the chicks safe.

This killdeer is pretending it is hurt.

Growing Up

Some chicks grow up very fast. Some are fully grown in only twenty days from **hatching**. Larger birds may take up to a year to become adults.

This albatross chick's soft **down molts** so adult feathers can grow.

Once the chicks are fully grown, they do not stay with their parents. They may live in bigger groups called flocks. Some **migrate** long distances every year.

Some kinds of geese can fly more than one thousand miles without stopping to rest.

Birds and Other Animals

		Fish
What they look like:	Bones inside body	all
	Number of legs	none
	Hair on body	none
	Scaly skin	most
	Wings	none
	Feathers	none
Where they live:	Live on land	none
	Live in water	all
How they are born:	Grow babies inside body	some
	Hatch from eggs	most
How babies get food:	Get milk from mother	none
	Parents bring food	none

Amphibians	Insects	Reptiles	Birds	Mammals
all	none	all	all	all
4 or none	6	4 or none	2	2 or 4
none	all	none	none	all
none	none	all	none	few
none	most	none	all	some
none	none	none	all	none
most	most	most	all	most
some	some	some	none	some
few	some	some	none	most
most	most	most	all	few
none	none	none	none	all
none	none	none	most	most

Glossary

beak   hard, pointed part of a bird's mouth

beg   to ask for something very strongly

cactus   (more than one are **cacti**) plant with no leaves that grows in deserts

down   small, soft, fluffy feathers that cover a chick's body and keep it warm

hatch   to be born from an egg

hatchling   name for a baby when it has just been born from an egg

lay   when an egg comes out of a female bird's body

migrate   to move from one place to another each year

molt   when chicks lose their old feathers and grow new adult ones

moss   small, soft, green plant that grows on soil, wood, or stone

predator   animal that will kill another animal for food or for its home

pretend   to do something that is not real

protect   to keep safe

reward   something given for being good or doing something well

seabird   bird that lives near the sea and gets food from it

yolk   part of an egg that is food for a baby animal

More Books to Read

Butterfield, Moira. *Quick, Quiet, & Feathered*. Austin, Tex.: Raintree Steck-Vaughn, 1997.

—. *Bright, Lively, and Loud*. Austin, Tex.: Raintree Steck-Vaughn, 1998.

Geiske, Ernestine. *Birds*. Des Plaines, Ill.: Heinemann Library, 1998.

Kalman, Bobbie. *Rainforest Birds*. New York: Crabtree Publishing Company, 1998.

Theodorou, Rod. *Heavy and Light*. Crystal Lake, Ill.: Rigby Interactive Library, 1996.

Index

animal groups   4, 28–29

beaks   6, 11–12, 15

chicks   5, 10–11, 13, 15–23, 25–27

down   26

eggs   5, 6–8, 10–11, 14, 17

egg tooth   11

feathers   6–8, 12–13, 22, 26

flocks   27

flying   7, 15, 18–20, 24–25, 27

food   10, 13–17, 20–21

hatchlings   11–14

migrating   27

molting   26

nests   7–8, 9, 13, 15–17, 19, 23–24

parents 12–15, 19, 20, 23–25, 27

predators   8, 22–25

wings   6, 18, 25